One Year
in New York
Darcel
Disappoints

VICTION
VICTION

Hello

When I moved to New York, I was blissfully naive; oblivious to the city's history and what was happening around me. I left behind family and friends in search of something different, and once I was living in the city I had all sorts of epiphanies, both big and small, about myself and my new home.

To remember these observations, I started putting my thoughts down in picture form on my blog, *Darcel Disappoints*. Some six hundred posts later, I've grouped together my favorites—along with some new insights—to encapsulate a single year of life. Over time, these observations have given me a fresh perspective on my life and those around me.

The posts are short stories; very short. They are one-frame observations that, together, paint an overview of life in a big city—and the inevitable loneliness that is sometimes supplanted by feeling like you are part of something bigger. From the mundane to the euphoric, the following pages show the full spectrum of *One Year in New York*.

Q&A
with Sarah
Andelman

Sarah Andelman is the founder of iconic Parisian store _colette_ and _Just An Idea_, her new creative venture. She and Craig Redman, creator of _Darcel Disappoints_, have collaborated on projects together for over a decade. Here, they discuss Darcel's beginnings and ongoing adventures.

Sarah

It has always been such a pleasure to work with you on various projects over the years; ironic considering how unhappy Darcel usually looks.

Craig

Darcel is the cynical side of me that I let creep out occasionally, hence the glum expression. Visually, I like that he's a grump in a bright and colorful illustrated world; it suggests that he's kind of at odds with what's around him. I made him unhappy initially less because he was depressed, and more because he felt let down by things.

When I moved to New York I wanted the city to be better, more like the fantastical idea I had of the city in my head from visiting, rather than the true grind of actually living here. I wanted to go to MoMA and walk away being staggered by what I saw, rather than being just ambivalent.

Of course it's ridiculous to have those kinds of expectations, and honestly making him grumpy was just more fun. Who isn't entertained by hearing a friend complain? I'd rather hear that than blind optimism.

Sarah

To be clear, you are Darcel right?

Craig

Pretty much. He's an exaggerated version of me for sure. He usually reacts to things in a more exuberant or exasperated way, but yeah, I'm sad to say we are one.

Sarah

You once explained to me that you designed Darcel as simply as possible. Why is that? I still think his wooden glasses are a nice touch and part of his chic elegance.

Craig

I had the idea for Darcel and designed him all in one day. I wanted him to be the quickest, most simple form I could think of; essentially a blank canvas where the activity in the illustration, and not the character, became the focus. He has an egg-like body and spaghetti-ish arms and legs because they were easier to draw in different positions, and a single eye purely because it looked better than two; but he looked a little bare, so giving him glasses gave him a specific identity and was a nod to the fashion world which he is peripherally a part of.

I also wanted him to be simple because I needed to be able to draw the ideas really quickly. An illustration can sometimes be a precious thing, something to be labored over; but I like the idea of making it fast and fuss-free, treating an illustration more like an Instagram post that you forget about an hour later.

Sarah

The drawings can seem easy or obvious, but the little moments you capture happen quickly in real life. Sometimes, we don't even notice them. To capture them, you need a little distance.

Craig

The illustrations really are mostly acknowledging those banal, simple moments that we usually don't even notice. It's fun to be able to reduce everyday activities to a single snapshot, capturing a small moment in time that alludes to something grander. They are things that a lot of people can relate to, and I think Darcel has been around for a while precisely because he is accessible. Even though he's an illustrated character, he doesn't ride a unicorn and live on a rainbow—he gets lonely, he struggles to pay the rent, he gets inappropriately drunk at times—he deals with the battles and grind of everyday life.

Sarah

Your ability to Darcel-ize the world is so unique!

Craig

I like the idea of visually reducing the world into basic shapes. Darcel himself is made from the simplest of forms, so the world he lives in needs to reflect that too. Often, the illustrations are simply Darcel doing something on, say, a red background - literally nothing else. So much can be said with just his expression and gestures. If I'm drawing a scene where he is out in the world, the sun will be reduced to a circle, and a building can be drawn with a couple of squares. It's the same with people - often, you can characterize someone purely by their hairstyle. It's fun to figure out how to do that in a way that is easily identifiable and looks great at the same time.

Sarah

I love it when he goes to see art.

Craig

It's funny how much his views on the art world have changed. When I first started drawing Darcel, I feel like I had extraordinarily high expectations for exhibitions because I'd just moved to New York and had unrealistic expectations about things. Places like The Met I had only read about or seen in movies, so I would go to an exhibition and think, "Oh, this is it?". Then, I'd draw up my thoughts, post it online, and people would think it was funny because I was dismissing an institution. It was really just me being incredibly naive. These days, he sees more niche shows and is generally more receptive to things because he's more aware. I love drawing Darcel at obscure galleries; it's really fun to draw, say, highly conceptual work in a Darcel-ized way.

Sarah

Did you ever watch Curb Your Enthusiasm and think, "This happened to me!"? It seems Darcel is an even more minute examination of reality. As a viewer you know the situation, it's something we can all relate to. It has happened to all of us, or it will.

Craig

I was a latecomer to Curb and when I finally watched it I thought, "Oh, I see!". Larry David is so perfect at representing everyday situations in really funny ways simply because he looks at them from a different perspective. That's what I try to do, too. A lot of the scenes I draw are moments we miss, or don't even think about in our everyday lives because they are so boring and commonplace. I try to linger on those and give them the platform they deserve.

Sarah

Did you ever meet someone in the subway or a restaurant who recognized you and complained as if he was personally attacked by Darcel irony?

Craig

Ha, no, but I often think friends might be silently asking themselves, "Is that me he's talking about?", and the answer is yes, it probably is. All my drawings come from observations of the world I inhabit, and that includes the actions of friends. For example, I did an illustration titled "What goes through the mind of the terminally late?" because we all have those friends who are never on time and I truly can't understand why. Hardly a sin, but I'd gotten sick of repeatedly standing on a street corner in the freezing cold waiting for them to arrive. I suppose this makes me wildly passive-aggressive?

Sarah

Do you think Darcel should travel more around the world?

Craig

The problem is that when I travel, the last thing I want to do is sit in front of a computer and draw. I always have good intentions of drawing up Darcel's adventures when I get home but it rarely happens. He does complain about being on an airplane a lot - does that count?

Sarah

Do you have notes on your phone where you list all the situations you'd like to draw? Do you draw them in the morning or evening?

Craig

I do. I have a list of ideas in my Notes ready to go. Some of them have been on there for years. If I'm going through a barren period I'll check my Notes, panic and think, "Oh God, it's only the lame ones left!".

Generally though, if I have an idea for an illustration, I'll do it within a few days. The ideas come out of everyday activities; like maybe when I'm walking to my studio in Brooklyn after lunch, I see a couple arguing and it will trigger an idea. The visual will start forming in my head and in the next couple of days, I'll try to draw it up. I try to do them quickly and painlessly. Darcel was always intended to be something that was simple and spontaneous for me, and I don't want it to ever become a drag.

January

January 1
Welcoming in the New Year the only way I know how.

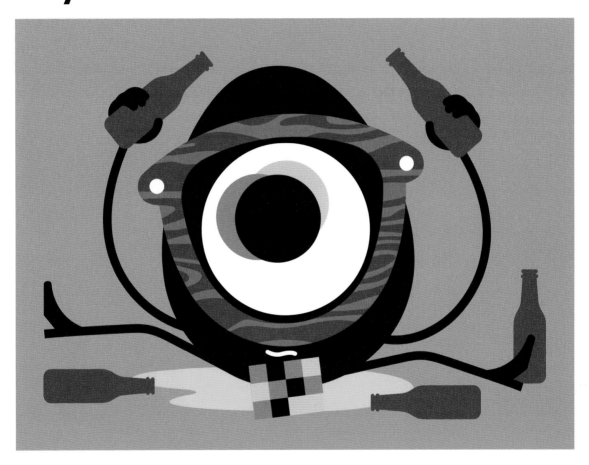

January 2
Hung-the-fuck-over.

2.24PM
< Notes
NEW YEAR'S RESOLUTIONS:
• Go to gym.
• Eat healthy.
• Be nicer.
• Work less.
• Call mom.
• No booze.
• Get ri
• Less
• Call
• More

January 4
The lies we tell ourselves.

January 9
Debauchery has a way of catching up with you.

January 12
Overall, winter in New York is true heaven.

January 16
New York Slip 'n Slide.

January 20
Everyone looks good during winter.

January 30
Slam dunk, it's the winter chunk.

February

Being alone sucks.

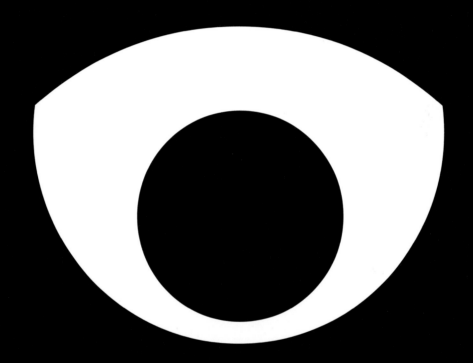

February 6
New York is a city for couples.

February 8

Friday night: no messages and no missed calls.

February 14
Another Valentine's, another night alone.

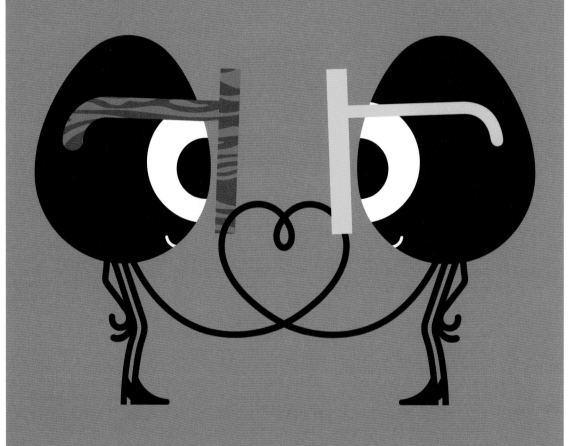

February 19
Misery needs company.

When 2 become 1, for 1 night only.

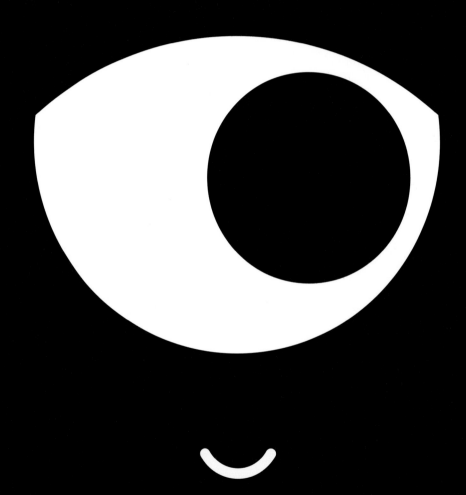

No more "I love you's."

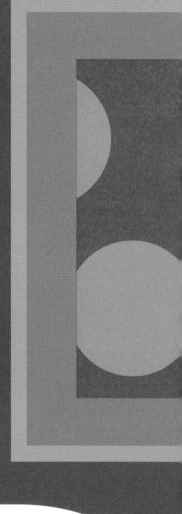

March

To live in New York is to be constantly conflicted.

March 7
Introducing Times Square, everyone's favorite vortex of hell.

March 12
Life in New York is a lot like crossing a busy street: keep moving or get run over.

March 16
When did Central Park become Disneyland?

March 20
All hail the NYC tourist photo pose.

Canal St couture.

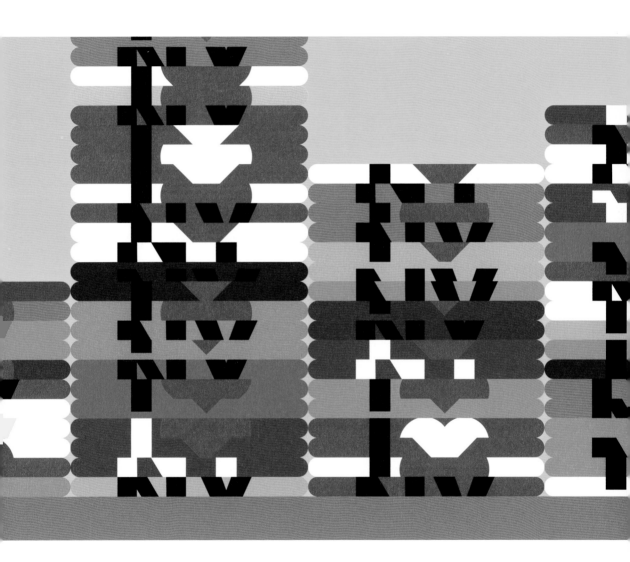

March 27
You learn in New York that no-one gives a fuck about anyone but themselves.

The real New York.

April

Wake up, check email, panic.

April 3
Daily drama.

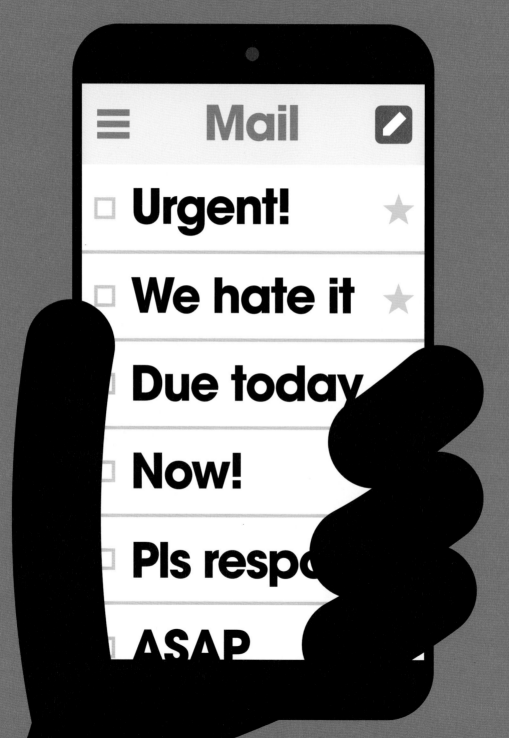

The relaxing walk to work.

You. Better. Work.

Fuck, I hate meetings.

Conference calls. WHY?

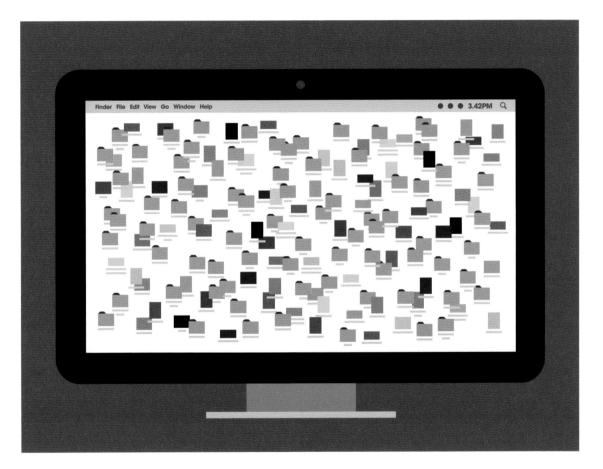

April 21
My life.

Beginning of the day.

End of the day.

April 30

Just once I'd like to feel invigorated by work, rather than broken by it.

May

The boring wait, at the boarding gate.

The trying times of a long-haul flight.

May 5
Paris shopping: fantasy vs. reality.

How many euros to get to Charles de Gaulle airport?!

Airplane food. Hell no.

May 20
Jet lag.

4:37
AM PM

June

June 8

I am not, and never will be, a morning person.

All hail the New York 20-minute line-up for a cup of coffee.

June 21

Gross. Oh wait, that's me.

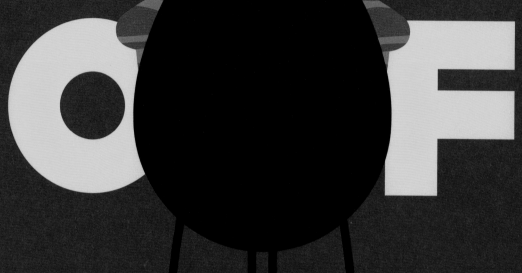

June 21
**A quiet day at MoMA
(with 300,000 others).**

June 21
One step too far, as always.

June 22
SHAME.

July

July 3
A last-minute, desperate attempt to not look disgusting for summer.

July 4
The day after.

July 10

Another summer, another season out of shape.

July 16

Summer in New York is fucked.

Dear heatwave: piss off.

June 23
I am not made for the heat.

New York rain.

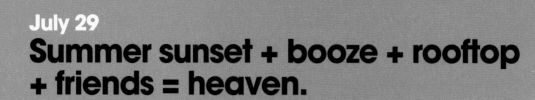

July 29
Summer sunset + booze + rooftop + friends = heaven.

August

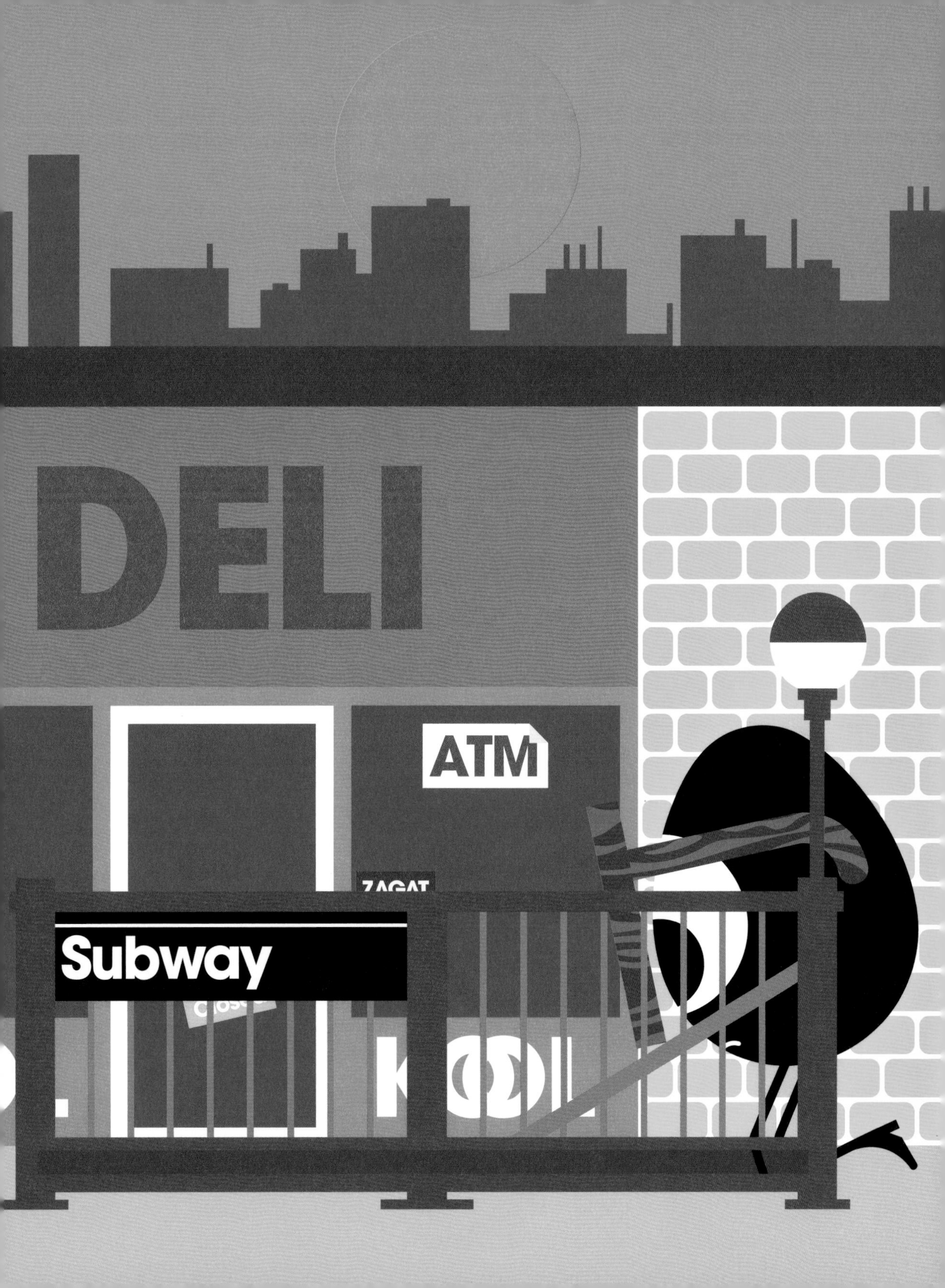
DELI
ATM
ZAGAT
Subway

August 9
Eating on the subway, I will never understand.

August 12
In New York, you're always 12 inches from someone.

August 19
I can never understand why people want to hang out in crowded bars. Give me a lonely dump any day.

August 24
The first piss after 3 beers is pure ecstasy.

August 28
I used to be fun.

Total happiness is arriving at the platform exactly as the train pulls in.

August 31
The L train.

September

September 7
New York Fashion Week,
here we go again.

Hours of lining up for minutes of fashion.

September 9
Looks.

September 10

One of these things is not like the others.

September 11
Front row fatality.

September 12
My usual view of the runway.

September 13
Shoes maketh the man.

September 14
Entry denied. I can't figure out why?

September 20
Fashion weak.

System

FANTASTIC MAN

POPEYE

VOGUE

October

People. Hate 'em.

October 8

If you don't have anything nice to say, come sit next to me.

Complaining about absolutely everything is thoroughly enjoyable.

I always thought I knew everything, but now I realize I know nothing.

I want to be invited, I just don't want to go.

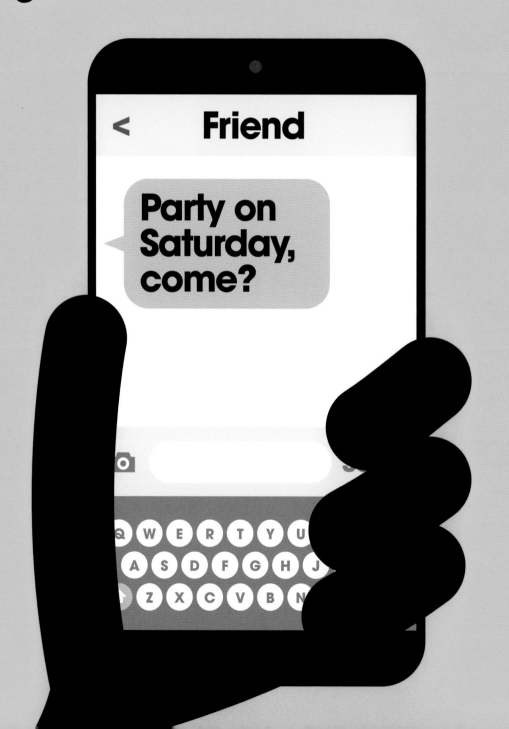

October 23

I'm constantly going to things I'm supposed to enjoy rather than what is actually enjoyable.

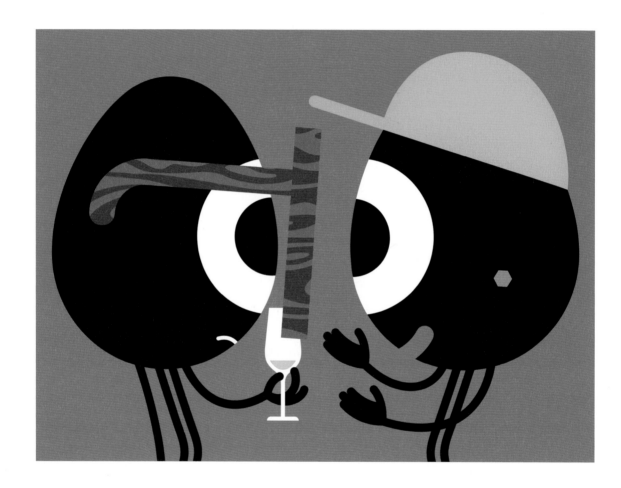

Complacency breeds banality.

Age is a bastard of a thing.

November

It just ain't fair, the cupboard is bare.

November 6

I have never mastered the art of eating out alone.

November 10
So tired of the New York restaurant game.

November 16
Food envy.

November 18

An unamused-bouche.

November 21

Live music in restaurants. No.

November 22
Communal tables. No.

November 27

That moment during dinner when everyone reaches for their phone.

November 30
It's always the booze that fucks you.

Bill

Food	20.00
Booze	40.00
Tax	5.34
Total	65.34

Have a nice day!

December

New York streets lined with Christmas trees bring even a seasoned cynic like me to my knees.

Quick trip to Art Basel Miami, didn't see any art.

December 5
Miami is not the place for me.

December 16
The last-minute Christmas gift panic and inevitable overspending to compensate for a shitty idea.

December 20
Canal St post office, 5 days before Christmas…what the fuck was I thinking?

December 22
This wasn't the kind of holiday bondage I had in mind.

December 24
Wrapped up in myself.

December 25

And a miserable Christmas to you too.

December 26
Post-Christmas vegetative state.

December 30

Summoning up the energy for New Year's is becoming harder every year.

December 31
Here we go again.

Thanks to Thomas, Bruce, Barb, Brett, Dean, Karl, Stevie, and Sarah.

©2019 viction:workshop ltd.
First published and edited by viction:workshop ltd.
Unit C, 7th Floor, Seabright Plaza,
9-23 Shell Street, North Point, Hong Kong
URL: www.victionary.com   Email: we@victionary.com
🔲 @victionworkshop
🐦 @victionary_
📷 @victionworkshop

Illustration © Darcel Disappoints / Craig Redman 2019
Text © Darcel Disappoints / Craig Redman 2019
www.darceldisappoints.com

ISBN 978-988-79033-3-8

Printed and bound in China